Grilled capsicum and fetta toasts

1
2 red capsicums

2
**170g tub
Persian fetta**

3
**1 small French
bread stick**

- Cut capsicums into quarters lengthways and place skin-side up under a preheated grill until skin blisters and blackens. Transfer grilled capsicum to a plastic bag to cool, then peel and discard skin.
- Cut capsicum into approximately 3cm pieces and place in a small bowl. Drain marinade from fetta and pour over capsicum pieces. Refrigerate fetta and capsicum separately.
- Cut bread stick into thin slices. Place bread slices on an oven tray in a single layer, spray lightly with cooking oil and cook under a preheated grill until lightly toasted. Turn bread slices and toast other side. Spread a little Persian fetta over toasts, then top with a piece of grilled capsicum. Season with freshly ground pepper and garnish with fresh oregano, if desired.

Makes about 20

Maple-glazed pumpkin wedges

1

1kg Queensland blue pumpkin

2

2 tblsp maple syrup

3

¼ cup chopped walnuts

- Remove the seeds from the pumpkin, but leave skin on, rinsing well to remove any dirt. Cut into large wedges.
- Place pumpkin wedges in a large, greased roasting pan, spray with cooking spray and bake in a 200C preheated oven for 30 minutes, turning wedges halfway during cooking.
- Remove roasting pan from oven, drizzle maple syrup over wedges and return to oven for 15 minutes. Sprinkle with walnuts and bake for a further 5 minutes or until pumpkin is tender and well glazed and nuts are lightly toasted.

Serves 4-6

Juicy corn with chives

1

4 whole corn cobs, in husks

2

60g soft butter

3

1 tblsp chopped fresh chives

- Remove silks from corn cobs but leave husks intact. Soak whole cobs in husks in a bowl of cold water for 1 hour, then drain.
- Combine butter and chives and mix well. Carefully peel back husks on corn cobs and spread kernels with chive butter.
- Lift husks back over kernels and secure at ends with string. Cook corn in husks on a barbecue for 15–20 minutes, turning often.

Serves 4

Blue cheese and thyme potatoes

1
8 small potatoes

2
75g Castello blue cheese

3
fresh thyme leaves

- Boil whole potatoes in a large saucepan for 10 minutes, drain.
- Transfer the par-cooked potatoes to a lightly oiled roasting pan, bake in a 210C preheated oven for 30 minutes or until light golden and tender.
- Cut a cross in the top of each potato, top with cheese and return to 210C oven for 5 minutes. Sprinkle with thyme and serve straightaway.

Serves 4

This recipe is best prepared as required.

Mushroom and tomato garlic toasts

1
375g large portobello mushrooms, halved

2
250g baby roma tomatoes, halved

3
270g packet garlic bread slices

- Cook the mushrooms and tomatoes in a heated, lightly oiled frypan or on a heated barbecue plate until lightly browned.
- Meanwhile, bake garlic bread as directed on the packet. Top garlic bread slices with mushroom and tomatoes, and season with salt and pepper.

Serves 4

Quick salmon dip

1
250g cream cheese, softened

2
¼ cup thousand island salad dressing

3
2 x 95g can sweet chilli flavoured salmon

● Beat cream cheese and salad dressing in a bowl with a wooden spoon until smooth and creamy, then stir in salmon. Serve with vegetable sticks or crackers of your choice.

Makes about 1½ cups

Cajun sweet potato chips

1
2 x medium (500g) orange sweet potatoes, peeled

2
3 tsp Cajun seasoning

3
1 tblsp olive oil

● Heat a large baking dish in a 220C preheated oven for 10 minutes. Cut sweet potatoes into chunky chips. Pat chips dry with paper towel, place in a large bowl with seasoning and oil and mix with clean hands to coat chips well.

● Add chips to heated baking dish in a single layer and bake in a 220C preheated oven for 20–25 minutes or until crisp and tender, turning them halfway through cooking time. Serve with sour cream, if desired.

Serves 4-6

Sesame snaps

1

1¹/₃ cups caster sugar

2

²/₃ cup glucose syrup

3

1 cup sesame seeds, lightly toasted

- Combine sugar and glucose syrup in a medium, heavy-based saucepan, place over a low heat until sugar is dissolved, stirring occasionally. Increase heat and boil without stirring for 7–8 minutes or until mixture reaches hard crack stage (150C on a sweets thermometer).

- Remove toffee from heat and stir in sesame seeds. Place a large sheet of baking paper on a flat heat-resistant surface (eg, stone bench top, large wooden board). Carefully pour mixture onto baking paper, place another piece of baking paper over mixture and roll with a rolling pin until about 2mm in thickness. Remove top sheet of baking paper, allow mixture to set and cool, then break into pieces.

Makes about 30 pieces

Creamy Dijon jacket potatoes

1

8 x 150g potatoes

2

250g spreadable cream cheese

3

2 tblsp Dijon mustard

- Scrub potatoes under cold water to remove any dirt, then wrap individually in aluminium foil. Place on oven rack in a 180C preheated oven and bake for 1 hour or until tender.
- Mix cream cheese and Dijon mustard in a bowl until well combined. Cut a cross in top of cooked potatoes and top with mustard cream cheese. Garnish with chives, if desired.

Serves 8

Barbecued prosciutto asparagus

1

2 bunches asparagus

2

8 thin slices prosciutto, approximately

3

200ml jar hollandaise sauce

- Trim ends from asparagus spears. Plunge asparagus into boiling water, then drain, refresh in cold water and drain again.
- Cut the prosciutto slices lengthways into approximately 2cm wide strips. Wrap prosciutto strips firmly around asparagus spears. Cook on a heated, greased barbecue plate until prosciutto is crisp and lightly browned. Serve with hollandaise sauce.

Serves 4-6

Home-style chips

1
3 large sebago potatoes

2
sunflower oil

3
salt

- Peel potatoes and cut into chunky chips. Place chips in a clean tea towel and pat well until thoroughly dry.
- Half fill a large saucepan or an electric deep-fryer with oil and heat until hot. Oil is ready when a cube of bread added to hot oil turns golden in about 30 seconds.
- Carefully add chips into hot oil and fry until crisp and golden. Remove chips from oil using tongs or a slotted spoon and drain well on paper towel. Season with salt and serve straightaway.

Serves 4

Toasted croissants with quick berry compote

1
300g frozen mixed berries, thawed

2
¾ cup icing sugar

3
4 large croissants

- Place thawed berries in a bowl, add the icing sugar and stir gently. Set aside until the sugar dissolves to form a syrup.
- Cut croissants in half and toast lightly. Serve with berry compote. This berry compote is also delicious over toasted waffles or warm pancakes.

Serves 4

Cheese and Vegemite twists

1
2 frozen puff pastry sheets, just thawed

2
2 tsp Vegemite, approximately

3
1 cup grated tasty cheese

- Lay 1 pastry sheet on a clean surface, spread with Vegemite and sprinkle with ¾ cup grated cheese.
- Top with another sheet of pastry, press down lightly with clean hands, then cut in half. Cut each piece into 2cm wide strips from the narrow side.
- Twist strips and place a few centimetres apart on baking paper-lined oven trays. Sprinkle with remaining grated cheese. Bake in a 220C preheated oven for 8–10 minutes or until golden. Cool on trays.

Makes about 16

Sweet potato crisps with tzatziki

1
2 medium sweet potatoes (any variety), peeled

2
1 litre vegetable oil, approximately

3
tzatziki dip

- Cut sweet potatoes into long thin slices* and pat dry with paper towel.
- Heat oil in a wok or deep-fryer. Deep-fry sweet potato slices in batches until lightly browned and crisp. Drain on paper towel and season to taste with salt and pepper.
- Serve sweet potato crisps with tzatziki dip.

Serves 4

*For best results use a mandolin-style slicer, available from specialty kitchen shops.

Chicken empanadas

1
4 cups chopped cooked chicken

2
375g jar enchilada sauce

3
1kg packet (5) frozen shortcrust pastry sheets, just thawed

- Mix chopped chicken and enchilada sauce together in a large bowl.
- Cut each pastry sheet into 9 rounds using a 9cm round cutter. Brush edges of rounds with water. Place a heaped teaspoon of chicken filling in centre of rounds then fold in half to enclose filling. Press the edges together to seal then mark with a fork.
- Place empanadas on baking paper-lined trays and bake in a 200C preheated oven for 12 minutes or until lightly browned. Serve warm with sour cream or extra enchilada sauce.

Makes 45

Seasoned potato wedges

1
1kg large brushed potatoes

2
1½ tsp MasterFoods Chicken Salt

3
1 tsp dried mixed herbs

- Scrub potatoes well under cold water to remove any dirt, then cut into wedges and pat dry with paper towel. Spread wedges in a single layer over a greased oven tray and spray potatoes lightly with cooking oil. Bake in a 220C preheated oven for 20 minutes. Remove from oven, turn wedges, spray again with the cooking oil and sprinkle with chicken seasoning and herbs. Return to 220C oven for a further 20–25 minutes or until wedges are crisp and golden. Accompany with sour cream, if desired.

Serves 4-6

Icy raspberry pops

1
1 cup frozen raspberries

2
½ cup caster sugar

3
375ml lemonade

- Place raspberries, sugar and 1 cup water in a saucepan and bring to the boil. Reduce heat and simmer uncovered for 10 minutes. Remove from heat, cool.
- Process raspberry mixture until smooth, then strain through a sieve to remove seeds. Pour mixture into a large jug and gradually stir in the lemonade. Set aside 15 minutes or until bubbles subside.
- Pour the raspberry mixture into 6 x 100ml popsicle moulds. Place in the freezer overnight. Remove the icy pops from the moulds just before serving.

Makes 6

Five spice chicken wings

1

¼ cup rice flour

2

2 tsp Chinese five spice powder

3

1kg chicken wings or drumsticks

- Combine rice flour and five spice powder in a plastic bag and season with salt and pepper. Add chicken wings to bag and shake to coat evenly in the spice mixture.
- Place seasoned chicken wings in a large, greased baking dish and spray with cooking oil spray. Bake in a 180C preheated oven for about 35–45 minutes or until wings are golden and cooked through. Serve with sweet chilli sauce, if desired.

Serves 4

Roasted red pepper spread

1

270g jar char-grilled capsicum

2

1 cup cashews, toasted

3

½ cup firmly packed basil leaves

- Drain the char-grilled capsicum and reserve 2 tablespoons of the oil marinade. Process the capsicum, reserved oil marinade, cashews and basil leaves in a food processor to form a thick paste. Transfer to a serving bowl and serve with Turkish bread or crackers.

Makes about 1 cup

Ginger ale

1

2 cups sugar

2

2 cups, peeled and thinly sliced ginger

3

soda water or mineral water

- Combine sugar, ginger and 2 cups water in medium saucepan. Stir over a medium heat until sugar is dissolved. Bring to the boil, then reduce heat and simmer uncovered for 8–10 minutes to form a thin syrup.
- Remove syrup from heat, cool to room temperature, then strain syrup and discard the ginger slices.
- Pour ¼ cup ginger syrup into glasses, add ice, if desired, then top up with mineral water. Serve with lime wedges.

Makes about 8 serving glasses

Two-tone icebergs

1

**2 tblsp each Cottee's
Apple Raspberry
and Coola
Concentrate Cordial**

2

**2 tblsp each Cottee's
Orange Crush
and Lemon Crush
Concentrate Cordial**

3

**lemonade, soda or
mineral water**

- Pour each of the four cordial flavours into separate jugs and stir ¾ cup water into each one.
- Half fill ice cube trays with the apple raspberry cordial, freeze until firm, then pour the orange crush cordial over frozen layer and return to freezer until orange layer is frozen. Half fill ice cube trays with coola cordial, freeze until firm, then pour the lemon crush cordial over frozen layer and return to freezer until lemon layer is frozen.
- Place icebergs in glasses and top up with lemonade, soda or mineral water.

Makes about 24 icebergs

Watermelon cocktail

1
1 cup diced watermelon

2
1 tblsp Triple Sec or Cointreau liqueur

3
squeeze lime juice

- Place watermelon, liqueur and lime juice in a blender or food processor, add a couple of handfuls of ice cubes and process until slushy. Pour into 2 small cocktail glasses and serve straightaway. Garnish with lime, if desired.

Makes 2

Pine mango bellini

1
1 mango, peeled and chopped

2
½ cup pineapple juice

3
dry sparkling wine, chilled

- Process the mango and pineapple juice in a food processor or blender until pureed. Strain the mixture through a sieve to remove any stringy pulp.
- Place about 2 tablespoons of the puree into champagne flutes and top up glasses with sparkling wine.

Makes 2

Guava sparkling cocktails

1

guava nectar

2

Cointreau or Grand Marnier

3

Pink sparkling wine

- One-third fill cocktail glasses with chilled guava nectar, add 10ml Cointreau to each of the glasses, then top up glasses with chilled sparkling wine. Serve immediately.

Pimms and blood orange spritzer

1

3 blood oranges

2

150ml Pimms No 1 Cup liqueur

3

lemonade, well chilled

- Cut 2 of the oranges in half and squeeze to extract juice. Slice the remaining orange thinly. Divide the orange juice, orange slices and Pimms between 4 tall glasses. Add ice cubes if desired, then top up glasses with lemonade. Serve straightaway.
Makes 4

Chocolate swirl meringues

1

100g dark chocolate, melted

2

3 eggwhites

3

¾ cup caster sugar

- Place the chocolate in a heat-resistant bowl, stand over a pan of simmering water (or microwave on medium for about 1 minute) until smooth and melted, stirring occasionally.
- Beat eggwhites in a bowl with an electric mixer until soft peaks form. Gradually add caster sugar and continue beating on high speed until the sugar is dissolved and the meringue is thick and glossy.
- Drizzle melted chocolate over meringue and partially fold in using a metal spoon to create a swirled effect. Place heaped teaspoons of meringue onto baking paper-lined oven trays.
- Bake in a 120C preheated oven for about 30 minutes or until dry. Turn oven off and allow the meringues to cool completely in the oven. These are delicious served with coffee.

Makes about 22

Berry frozen yoghurt

1
2 cups frozen mixed berries

2
¼ cup icing sugar

3
850g tub creamy Greek-style strawberry yoghurt

• Process the frozen mixed berries in a food processor until finely chopped. Add the icing sugar and yoghurt and process again until the mixture is smooth.
• Transfer the fruit/yoghurt mixture to a loaf pan, cover and freeze a few hours or until mixture is just frozen.
• Break up the frozen mixture, return to food processor and process once more until smooth. Return mixture to loaf pan and freeze overnight. Remove frozen yoghurt from freezer 15–20 minutes before serving to allow it to soften slightly before scooping into bowls.

Serves 6

Choc-strawberry flower cupcakes

1
450g packet Green's Strawberry Choc Cupcakes

2
250g punnet small strawberries

3
12 pink Smarties

• Prepare and bake cupcake mixture as directed on packet. Prepare frosting mix as directed on packet.
• Spread frosting over cooled cupcakes. Slice strawberries thinly. Fan slices in a circular pattern over each cupcake to resemble flowers and place a Smartie in the centre of each one.

Makes 12

Cupcakes can be baked and frosted a day ahead. Store them in an airtight container. Decorate with strawberry flowers up to 1 hour before serving.

Crispy choc truffles

1
100ml thickened cream

2
200g dark chocolate, chopped

3
2 cups Coco Pops

- Place the cream and chocolate in a heat-resistant bowl. Stand bowl over a pan of simmering water and stir until mixture is smooth and melted. Remove bowl from heat, stand at room temperature, or refrigerate in hot weather until mixture cools and thickens.
- Spread the Coco Pops over a shallow tray. Toss teaspoons of the chocolate mixture in the cocoa pops and roll into balls. Place in a single layer in an airtight container and refrigerate for several hours or until firm.

Makes about 26

S'mores

1
digestive biscuits

2
marshmallows

3
milk or dark chocolate

- Place a layer of the digestive biscuits on a baking paper-lined oven tray. Top each biscuit with two marshmallows and two squares of chocolate.
- Cook in a 170C preheated oven for 5–10 minutes until marshmallows have softened and chocolate is just melted. Remove from oven, place another biscuit on top and press lightly.

Makes about 12
To make camp fire and BBQ s'mores, sandwich two biscuits together with two marshmallows and two chocolate squares. Wrap in foil and place in hot coals or on a BBQ hot plate until melted.

Honeycomb

1

**¹/₃ cup
golden syrup**

2

**1 cup caster
sugar**

3

**3 tsp
bicarbonate of
soda, sifted**

- Grease a 20cm square cake pan and line with baking paper to cover base and extend up sides of pan.
- Combine golden syrup, sugar and 1 tablespoon water in a medium saucepan. Stir mixture over a low heat, without boiling, until sugar is dissolved. Increase heat and bring to the boil. Boil, without stirring, for 3–4 minutes or until syrup is golden and reaches hard crack stage (148C on a sweets thermometer).
- Remove saucepan from heat, place on a wooden board or insulated heat mat. Quickly stir through the sifted soda with a wooden spoon, then spoon the foamy mixture into the prepared pan, avoiding spreading as this will cause mixture to deflate. Allow honeycomb to cool and set, then remove from pan and cut into chunks.

Makes about 20 pieces

Rocky road ice-cream cones

1

2 litres vanilla ice-cream

2

250g rocky road, roughly chopped

3

8 vanilla and chocolate waffle cones

- Stand ice-cream at room temperature until softened slightly. Spoon the ice-cream into a large bowl and stir in rocky road.
- Return ice-cream to clean ice-cream container, cover and freeze for several hours or overnight until firm.
- Spoon the ice-cream into waffle cones to serve.

Makes about 8 cones

Cinnamon sugar soldiers

1

4 x 59g eggs

2

8 thick bread slices

3

cinnamon sugar

- Break eggs into a bowl, add 2 tablespoons of water and beat well with a fork. Cut crusts from bread slices, then cut each piece into 3 strips.
- Dip bread pieces in beaten eggs, then shallow-fry a few pieces at a time in a heated, oiled frypan.
- Drain on paper towel, then sprinkle with cinnamon sugar and serve straightaway.

Serves 4

Apricot pies

1
2 x 400g can pie apricots

2
2 tblsp Demerara sugar

3
3 sheets butter puff pastry

- Mix the pie apricots in a bowl with 1 tablespoon of the sugar.
- Cut each pastry sheet into 4 squares. Press pastry squares into a greased 12-hole standard, non-stick muffin pan. Spoon apricot mixture into pastry cases, then fold pastry over filling and press seams together to seal.
- Sprinkle remaining sugar over pies and bake in a 210C preheated oven for 15–20 minutes or until pastry is puffed and golden brown. Serve with cream or ice-cream.

Makes 12

Ginger and walnut bites

1
250g block cream cheese, softened

2
100g (½ cup) crystallised ginger, finely chopped

3
¾ cup walnuts, toasted and finely chopped

- Place cream cheese in a bowl and stir in ginger.
- Refrigerate mixture for 1 hour or until firm.
- Roll heaped teaspoons of cream cheese mixture in chopped walnuts to coat evenly.

Makes about 20
Ginger and walnut bites will keep for up to 1 week in an airtight container in refrigerator.

Turkish and macadamia delight

1

2 x 180g blocks premium white cooking chocolate

2

200g Turkish delight, chopped

3

¾ cup macadamia nuts, toasted and roughly chopped

• Grease a 7cm x 26cm bar pan and line with enough baking paper to cover base and extend up sides of pan.

• Break white chocolate into pieces and place in a heat-resistant bowl. Stand the bowl over a pan of simmering water until chocolate is just melted, stirring occasionally. Remove from heat, cool, then stir in Turkish delight and macadamias. Spread mixture into prepared pan and refrigerate for several hours or until firm.

• Remove from the fridge, stand at room temperature for about 30 minutes before cutting into 8mm slices. Use a warm knife to make slicing easier.

Makes about 26 slices

Slices will keep in an airtight container in the fridge for up to 2 weeks.

Anzac ice-cream slice

1

300g pkt Anzac biscuits

2

2 litres vanilla ice-cream

3

2 tblsp finely chopped crystallised ginger

• Place Anzac biscuits in a plastic bag and crush roughly with a rolling pin.

• Spoon ice-cream into a large bowl, allow it to soften slightly, then add the ginger and half the crushed Anzac biscuits and mix to combine.

• Grease an 18cm x 28cm rectangular pan and line with enough baking paper to cover base and extend up sides of pan. Sprinkle half the remaining crushed biscuits over the base of prepared pan, top with ice-cream mixture, spreading it evenly. Sprinkle with the remaining crushed Anzac biscuits. Cover with plastic wrap and freeze overnight until firm. Cut slice into squares to serve.

Serves 10

Chocolate marshmallow fudge

1

250g packet pink and white marshmallows

2

30g butter

3

200g dark cooking chocolate, chopped

- Grease a 12cm × 22cm loaf pan and line with baking paper to cover base and extend up sides of pan.
- Place the white marshmallows, butter and 1 tablespoon water in a small saucepan, stir over a low heat until marshmallows are melted (or microwave on medium for about 1 minute).
- Remove from heat, add chocolate, stir until it melts and mixture is smooth. Roughly chop pink marshmallows and stir through chocolate mixture. Spread mixture into prepared pan, refrigerate for several hours or until firm. Lift fudge from pan with lining paper and cut into small squares to serve.

Makes about 18 pieces

White chocolate roughs

1

1 cup shredded coconut

2

180g block premium white cooking chocolate

3

15g copha

- Spread coconut over an oven tray. Place in a 180C preheated oven for 5 minutes or until light golden. Remove from oven.
- Break white chocolate into pieces and place in a heat-resistant bowl with copha. Stand bowl over a pan of simmering water (do not allow water to touch base of bowl), stir until mixture is smooth and just melted. Remove melted chocolate from heat, stir in toasted coconut. Spread heaped teaspoonfuls of mixture into 4cm rounds on foil or baking paper-lined trays. Allow to set at room temperature, or refrigerate in warm weather.

Makes 18

Mushroom and fetta omelette

Serves 1

1
140g marinated fetta cheese

2
75g button mushrooms, sliced

3
2 x 59g eggs

• Heat 1–2 teaspoons of oil from the marinated fetta cheese in a small non-stick frypan, add mushrooms and sauté until tender. Remove mushrooms from the frypan and set aside. Keep frypan warm over medium heat. Lightly beat the eggs together with 1 tablespoon of cold water.

• Pour egg mixture into heated, greased small frypan and cook over a medium heat, drawing edges of mixture toward centre so that unset mixture flows to the edge of pan.

• When omelette is almost set, sprinkle sautéed mushrooms and crumbled fetta cheese over half the omelette, then flip unfilled side of omelette over filling. Stand over low heat for a further minute to allow filling to heat through. Slide onto serving plate and then serve straightaway.

Makes 1

Labne, pear and watercress salad

1

370g jar marinated labne*

2

1 bunch watercress

3

2 firm pears, sliced

- Drain and reserve the oil marinade from labne.
- Trim stems from watercress. Rinse leaves under cold water, then pat dry with paper towel and break into small sprigs.
- Arrange watercress sprigs on a large serving platter, top with labne and sliced pear and drizzle with a little of the reserved labne marinade.

Serves 4-6

*Labne is a type of cream cheese made from strained yoghurt and formed into balls. It's available from delicatessens.

Spicy chicken drumsticks

1

250g apricot jam

2

35g pkt taco seasoning

3

8 chicken drumsticks

- Mix the jam and taco seasoning together in a bowl.
- Coat drumsticks evenly in the seasoned jam mixture and place onto a baking paper-lined baking tray. Bake in a 180C preheated oven for 30–35 minutes or until the chicken is golden and cooked through. Serve chicken hot or cold with salad of your choice.

Serves 4

Mexican-style eggs

1

425g can Mexican-style chilli beans

2

400g can crushed tomatoes with roasted capsicum

3

3 large eggs

- Combine beans and tomatoes in a medium frypan and bring to the boil. Reduce to a simmer and use the back of a spoon to make 3 hollows in the mixture.
- Break eggs into the hollows, cover frypan with a lid and cook for a further 3 minutes or until eggs are just set. Garnish with chopped parsley and serve with toast or crusty bread.

Serves 2-3

This recipe is best prepared as required.

Char-grilled asparagus and mozzarella salad

1

2 bunches asparagus

2

110g buffalo mozzarella

3

1 lemon, halved

- Cook asparagus spears on a heated, greased barbecue until lightly browned and just tender. Tear buffalo mozzarella into small pieces. Arrange asparagus on a serving plate, top with mozzarella and a good squeeze of lemon juice. Serve seasoned with freshly ground pepper.

Serves 4

Orange and radish salad

1

4 medium oranges, sliced

2

3-4 radishes, thinly sliced

3

small handful mint leaves

- Cut the rind and pith from three oranges, and then cut into segments. Halve the remaining orange and squeeze to extract juice.
- Arrange the orange segments and radish slices on a serving plate.
- Sprinkle with the mint leaves and drizzle with a little orange juice. Season with pepper.

Serves 4

This recipe is best prepared as required.

Barbecue prawns with wasabi mayonnaise

1

750g green king prawns (20)

2

½ cup mayonnaise

3

1 tsp wasabi paste

- Peel and devein prawns, leaving tails intact. Thread each prawn, tail-end first, onto a small bamboo skewer (as pictured).
- Combine the mayonnaise and wasabi in a small bowl.
- Cook the prawns on a heated, lightly oiled barbecue plate until lightly browned and just cooked through, turning occasionally. Serve barbecue prawns with the wasabi mayonnaise.

Serves 4-6

Lamb and caramelised onion samosas

1
400g lamb mince

2
280g jar caramelised onion and rosemary salsa (see note)

3
1kg packet (5) frozen shortcrust pastry sheets

• Add the lamb mince to a heated, non-stick frypan, stir over heat until mince is browned all over, breaking any lumps. Stir in the caramelised onion and rosemary salsa and remove mince from heat. Cool.

• Cut each pastry sheet into 9 rounds using an 8cm cutter. Place a heaped teaspoon of lamb filling into the centre of each pastry round. Brush edge of pastry rounds with a little water, fold in half to enclose filling and press edges to seal, then roll and fold edges to create a decorative effect, if desired.

• Deep-fry samosas, about 6 at a time, in hot oil until golden. Drain on paper towel and serve with extra caramelised onion and rosemary salsa, if desired.

Makes 45

Samosas can be cooked a day ahead. Refrigerate in an airtight container and reheat in a moderate oven. Freeze for up to 1 month.
Note: We used Always Fresh antipasto (caramelised onion and rosemary).

Asparagus crostini

1

2 bunches asparagus, ends trimmed

2

6 slices pizza bruschettina bread

3

250g fresh ricotta

- Char-grill the asparagus spears on a heated, lightly oiled barbecue plate or pan-fry in a greased non-stick frypan until lightly browned and just tender.
- Lightly toast the pizza bruschettina bread.
- Spread ricotta over toasted bread and top with char-grilled asparagus. Season with freshly cracked pepper and accompany with lemon wedges, if desired.

Makes 6

Pizza bruschettina bread is available in packets from the bakery section in supermarkets. You can substitute any Italian-style bread, if preferred.

Chicken Madras rolls

1

600g chicken mince

2

2 tblsp Madras curry paste

3

3 sheets frozen puff pastry, just thawed

- Mix chicken mince and curry paste together until well combined. Cut pastry sheets in half. Spread approximately $^1/_3$ cup of the mince mixture evenly along one edge of each pastry strip.

- Brush the opposite edges with a little water, then roll up to enclose filling and form long rolls. Cut each roll into 4 pieces.

- Place rolls on baking-paper lined oven trays, spray lightly with cooking spray and bake in a 200C preheated oven for 15–20 minutes until golden and cooked through. Serve with plain yoghurt or sauce of your choice.

Makes about 24

Spinach baked eggs

1
60g baby spinach leaves

2
4 x 59g eggs

3
¼ cup grated colby cheese

- Steam or microwave spinach leaves until just wilted, drain well. Divide spinach between 2 x ¾-cup capacity greased ramekin dishes. Break 2 eggs into each dish, sprinkle with grated cheese.
- Place ramekins on an oven tray and bake in a 180C preheated oven for 15–20 minutes or until cheese is lightly browned and eggs are set. Season with salt and pepper and serve with wholegrain toast.

Serves 2

Tandoori turkey rissoles

1
500g turkey mince

2
1 cup soft fresh breadcrumbs

3
2 tblsp tandoori paste

- Place the turkey mince, breadcrumbs and tandoori paste in a large bowl and mix with clean hands until thoroughly combined. Shape ¼-cup quantities into patties. Place turkey patties on a baking-paper lined oven tray, spray with cooking oil and bake in a 180C preheated oven for 25 minutes or until cooked through. Serve with salad and yoghurt or tzatziki dip.

Serves 4

Turkey rissoles can be prepared several hours ahead. Keep them covered in refrigerator and cook as required.

Salmon and pesto quinoa

1
¾ cup quinoa

2
2 tblsp basil pesto

3
2 x 95g cans salmon with lemon and pepper

- Place quinoa and 1½ cups cold water in a medium saucepan and bring to the boil. Reduce heat to low, cover and simmer 10–12 minutes or until water has been absorbed and quinoa is tender. Remove from heat, stand covered 5 minutes.
- Transfer cooked quinoa to a large bowl, stir in pesto until well combined then gently fold in salmon. Serve warm or chilled. Accompany with lemon wedges, if desired.

Serves 2

Tomato and basil salad

1
800g mixed tomatoes*

2
1 cup firmly packed fresh basil leaves

3
½ cup French vinaigrette-style dressing

- Slice the larger tomatoes thickly and cut the smaller ones in half. Arrange on a platter.
- Process basil leaves and salad dressing in a food processor or blender until smooth. Drizzle basil dressing over tomatoes. Season salad with freshly ground pepper and garnish with extra basil leaves, if desired. Serve straightaway.

Serves 4

*Mixed tomatoes are available in punnets from some supermarkets and greengrocers. Alternatively, choose your own variety.

Sweet kumara frittata

1

1 medium (500g) kumara (orange sweet potato), sliced

2

6 x 59g eggs

3

3 green shallots, thinly sliced

- Add kumara slices to a heated, lightly oiled, 26cm non-stick frypan, cover and cook over a low-medium heat for 10 minutes, stirring often, until just tender.
- Whisk the eggs in a large bowl, season with salt and pepper and stir in shallots. Spread kumara slices evenly in frypan, then pour in the beaten egg mixture.
- Cook over a low-medium heat for 5 minutes or until almost set. Place the pan (but not handle) under a preheated grill and cook until the frittata is set and the top is golden. Stand in pan for a few minutes, then slide onto a plate. Cut into wedges and serve with sweet chilli sauce, if desired.

Serves 4-6

This recipe is best prepared as required.

Salami and potato frittata

1

300g potatoes

2

75g shaved salami, roughly chopped

3

4 x 59g eggs

- Peel potatoes and cut into 1cm dice. Add to a heated, greased small 21cm frypan and sauté over a low-medium heat for 8–10 minutes or until potatoes are golden and just tender.
- Add salami, and sauté for 2 minutes. Whisk eggs and season with pepper. Pour eggs over potato and salami in frypan, cook over a low-medium heat for 8–10 minutes until almost set.
- Place frypan (but not handle) under a preheated grill for a few minutes or until frittata is set and golden. Serve in wedges with salad.

Serves 2-4

Korma kumara soup

1

1kg kumara (orange sweet potato), peeled and chopped

2

2 tblsp korma paste

3

1 litre vegetable stock

- Add kumara and korma paste to a large, lightly greased, deep pan and stir over heat for 1–2 minutes until fragrant.
- Add vegetable stock and bring to the boil. Reduce heat and simmer covered for 30 minutes or until kumara is tender.
- Blend or process soup in batches until smooth. Return to saucepan and heat through. Serve with a swirl of cream or sour cream.

Serves 4-6

Soup can be made in advance. Keep covered in the refrigerator for several days or freeze for up to 3 months. Reheat as required.

Smoked salmon and fetta on pumpernickel

1
150g marinated fetta cheese

2
4 slices pumpernickel bread

3
4 slices smoked salmon

- Mash fetta cheese with a fork and spread over pumpernickel bread. Top each bread slice with a piece of smoked salmon.
- Season with freshly ground pepper and serve with lemon wedges, if desired.

Makes 2-4

Eggplant and fetta stacks

1
2 medium (350g) eggplant

2
200g marinated fetta cheese

3
fresh basil leaves

- Cut eggplant into approximately 1.5cm thick slices. Crumble the fetta cheese and reserve the oil marinade.
- Add eggplant slices to a heated, oiled non-stick frypan and cook until browned on both sides and just tender.
- Layer the eggplant slices, crumbled fetta and basil leaves on serving plates. Drizzle with reserved marinade and season with freshly ground black pepper. Serve with crusty bread.

Serves 4

Marinated fetta is available from delicatessens and supermarkets.

Jacket potatoes with topping

1

4 x 200g potatoes

2

**small tub
tabouli salad**

3

**200g twin pack
hummus and
tzatziki dip**

- Scrub potatoes under cold water and pat dry with paper towel. Prick potato skins with fork then wrap each potato in foil.
- Bake in 180C preheated oven for 1 hour or until tender. Alternatively, place unwrapped potatoes directly on microwave turntable and microwave on high for 8–10 minutes until tender.
- Cut a deep cross in the top of each potato, fill with tabouli and top with hummus and tzatziki dip.

Serves 4

Entree

Quince and camembert puffs

1
**1 sheet puff
pastry**

2
**125g round
camembert cheese**

3
**¼ cup
quince paste,
approximately**

- Cut pastry sheet into 16 squares. Press a 5cm round cookie cutter lightly in the centre of pastry squares, without cutting all the way through, to create a border. Place pastry squares on a lightly greased oven tray.
- Cut the camembert round into quarters, then cut each quarter into 4. Spoon about ½ teaspoon quince paste over the marked round on each pastry square and top each one with a piece of camembert.
- Spray with cooking oil spray and bake in a 200C preheated oven for 10 minutes or until golden. Season puffs with freshly ground pepper and garnish with fresh herbs of your choice. Serve warm as a starter.

Makes 16

Puffs can be cooked several hours ahead. Cool and store in an airtight container in the refrigerator. Reheat in a 150C preheated oven just prior to serving.

Asparagus, haloumi and prosciutto starters

1

12 asparagus spears

2

180g packet haloumi

3

3-4 thin slices prosciutto

- Cut asparagus spears into 12cm lengths, place into a heat-resistant dish, cover with boiling water, stand 2 minutes then drain.
- Cut haloumi into 12 thin slices. Pan-fry slices in a heated, greased frypan until golden on both sides. Remove from heat, drain on paper towel. Lay an asparagus spear on each slice of cooked haloumi and wrap a strip of prosciutto around each serving.
- Pan-fry in a heated, greased frypan or on a greased barbecue plate until prosciutto is crisp. Serve straightaway.

Makes 12

Prosciutto-wrapped prawns

1

24 green king prawns

2

12 thin slices prosciutto

3

garlic aioli

- Shell and devein prawns, leaving the tails intact. Cut prosciutto slices in half lengthways.
- Wrap a strip of prosciutto firmly around each prawn. Cook prosciutto-wrapped prawns on a heated, greased barbecue plate or in a non-stick frypan until prosciutto is light golden and prawns are cooked through, turning occasionally. Serve with garlic aioli.

Makes 24

Baked herb camembert

1

200g camembert

2

4-6 small fresh thyme sprigs

3

1 clove garlic, very thinly sliced

- Cut top off camembert round, sprinkle with thyme leaves and garlic slices, then replace camembert top and wrap in two layers of baking paper.
- Bake in a 180C preheated oven for 6-8 minutes until the camembert is warmed. Serve with toasted bread rounds or crackers.

Serves 4-6

Beetroot dip

1

450g can of baby beets

2

150g roasted cashews

3

½ cup grated parmesan cheese

- Drain baby beets and reserve juice. Place baby beets, cashews and parmesan cheese in a food processor and process until it forms a smooth, thick paste.
- Thin the mixture to desired consistency with a little reserved juice (about ¼ cup) and process until well combined. Serve with crackers or vegetable sticks of your choice.

Makes about 1 ½ cups

Smoked salmon pate

1

100g smoked salmon slices, roughly chopped

2

250g cream cheese, softened

3

grated rind and juice from 1 lemon

- Process smoked salmon, cream cheese, lemon rind and juice in a food processor until smooth.
- Line a 375ml capacity mould with plastic wrap. Spoon salmon mixture into prepared mould, cover with plastic wrap and refrigerate overnight.
- Turn the pate onto a serving plate and remove the plastic lining. Serve the pate with melba toasts, biscuits or crackers of your choice.

Pigs in blankets

1

1kg cocktail frankfurts

2

2 sheets puff pastry

3

1 egg, lightly beaten

- Cut one sheet of pastry into 4 even strips, then cut each strip into 4 to give 16 squares. Repeat with the remaining pastry sheet.
- Lay cocktail frankfurts diagonally across pastry squares, lift pastry sides over frankfurts and secure with toothpicks.
- Brush beaten egg lightly over top of pastry coverings. Place about 5cm apart on greased oven trays and bake in a 200C preheated oven for about 10 minutes or until light golden. Remove toothpicks to serve. Accompany with tomato sauce for dipping.

Make 32

Cream cheese and walnut dates

1

**250g (about 16)
fresh dates**

2

**⅓ cup spreadable
cream cheese**

3

**¼ cup walnut
pieces**

- Cut a slit in dates and remove seeds.
- Mix the cream cheese until it is smooth.
- Spoon a little cream cheese into each date and top with walnuts. Serve lightly dusted with cinnamon sugar, if desired.

Makes about 16

Entree

Cheesy basil rounds

1

1 small French bread stick

2

150g tub chunky basil dip

3

150g mozzarella, cut into thick strips

- Cut bread stick diagonally into approximately 1.5cm thick slices and toast lightly on each side under a preheated grill.
- Spread toasted bread slices liberally with basil dip, then top with mozzarella strips. Return to preheated grill until cheese is melted. Garnish with fresh basil leaves, if desired, and serve immediately.

Makes 10–12 slices

Spinach and fetta bread cases

1
1 loaf sliced wholemeal bread (approx 22 slices)

2
200g baby spinach and fetta dip

3
6 cherry tomatoes, quartered

- Trim crusts from bread slices, then roll thinly with a rolling pin and cut into rounds with a 7cm cutter.
- Press bread rounds into greased mini muffin pans. Spray with cooking spray and bake in a 180C preheated oven for 10 minutes or until crisp and golden.
- Spoon the spinach dip evenly into bread cases, top with cherry tomato pieces and season with freshly ground pepper.

Makes about 22

Caramelised onion and goat's cheese bites

1
24 bite-size vol au vents

2
280g jar caramelised onion

3
75g goat's cheese, approximately

- Fill vol au vent cases with caramelised onion, then top them with a little goat's cheese.
- Place on an oven tray and bake in a 180C preheated oven for 8–10 minutes until heated through. Garnish with fresh herbs, if desired. Serve warm.

Makes 24

Warm asparagus and haloumi salad

1
3 bunches asparagus, ends trimmed

2
180g haloumi

3
1-2 tblsp lemon and oregano salad dressing

- Cut asparagus in half diagonally. Plunge into a large pan of boiling water for 30 seconds then drain. Refresh under cold water and drain again.
- Cut haloumi into small cubes and pan-fry in a heated, lightly oiled, large non-stick frying pan until light golden. Drain on paper towel.
- Toss asparagus spears with salad dressing. Place on a serving plate and scatter haloumi cubes on top. Season with cracked pepper, if you like.

Serves 4-6

Baked figs with blue cheese and prosciutto

1
4 small– medium figs

2
4 thin slices prosciutto, approximately

3
60g blue cheese, cut into small pieces

- Cut figs into quarters. Cut prosciutto slices in half lengthways, then cut each piece into 2.
- Top each fig wedge with a piece of blue cheese, wrap in strip of prosciutto and secure with a toothpick.
- Place wrapped figs on an oven tray and cook under a preheated grill for 1–2 minutes until prosciutto becomes crisp and cheese starts to melt.

Makes 16 serve warm.

Smashed chats with garlic and rosemary

1

1kg chat potatoes

2

2 tsp chopped fresh rosemary

3

1-2 tblsp garlic-infused olive oil

- Cook chats in a large pan of boiling water for 10–12 minutes or until almost tender, then drain and cool slightly.
- Transfer chats to a large roasting pan, gently squash with the back of spoon, then sprinkle with rosemary and drizzle with garlic oil.
- Season with salt and pepper and bake in a 220C preheated oven for 25–30 minutes until chats become crisp and golden.

Serves 6

Nachos chicken strips

1

500g chicken breast fillets

2

175g pkt Nacho-flavoured corn chips

3

1 egg, lightly beaten

- Cut chicken breast fillets lengthways into thin slices.
- Process corn chips in a food processor until finely crumbed. Beat egg with 1 tablespoon of cold water in a small shallow dish.
- Dip chicken pieces in beaten egg, then toss in corn chip crumbs to coat evenly. Place on a baking paper-lined tray, spray with cooking oil and bake in a 200C preheated oven for 10 minutes. Turn chicken pieces over and bake for a further 5–10 minutes until coating is crisp and chicken is cooked through. Serve with salsa and sour cream, if desired.

Serves 4-6

Lamb with pea puree and roast parsnip

1

4 medium parsnips, peeled

2

4 x 120g lean lamb steaks

3

500g frozen minted peas

- Cut parsnips in quarters lengthways, place in a lightly oiled roasting dish and bake in a 200C preheated oven for about 30 minutes or until they're tender and golden, turning them occasionally during the cooking time.

- Pan-fry lamb steaks in a heated, lightly greased, non-stick frypan for about 4 minutes on each side or until cooked to your liking. Remove steaks from heat and rest in a warm spot for about 1–2 minutes.

- Meanwhile, add peas to a large saucepan of boiling water. Boil for 3–5 minutes, then drain, reserving 1 tablespoon of the cooking water. Transfer peas with reserved cooking water to a food processor, season with salt and pepper and process to form a coarse puree. Divide hot pea puree between 4 serving plates, top with lamb steaks and roasted parsnip. Season with freshly ground pepper and accompany with mint jelly or mint sauce, if desired.

Serves 4

Maple and mustard glazed pork

1

4 pork sirloin steaks

2

¹/₃ cup maple syrup

3

2 tblsp wholegrain mustard

- Pan-fry pork steaks in a heated, non-stick frypan for about 4 minutes on each side or until just cooked through. Remove steaks from pan.
- Drain excess fat from pan, add maple syrup, mustard and ¼ cup water. Simmer 2–3 minutes until reduced and thickened slightly.
- Return steaks to pan, turning them to coat in maple mustard sauce and heat through. Serve with vegetables of your choice.

Serves 4

Best prepared as required.

Barbecued fish with olive avocado salsa

1

4 fish cutlets (we used blue eye cod)

2

1 firm, ripe avocado, diced

3

175g marinated split green olives*

- Cook fish cutlets on a heated, greased barbecue plate for 3–5 minutes on each side or until lightly browned and just cooked through.
- Combine avocado and marinated olives in a bowl and season with freshly ground pepper.
- Serve fish topped with olive avocado salsa. Accompany with lemon cheeks and a leafy salad.

Serves 4

*Split green olives are available from some delicatessens. If they're unavailable, use any variety of marinated, pitted green olives. Cut in half before mixing with avocado.

Surf 'n' turf

1

4 scotch fillet steaks

2

375g king prawns, peeled and deveined

3

200g jar bearnaise sauce, warmed

- Pan-fry or barbecue steaks until cooked to your liking.
- Meanwhile, sauté prawns in a heated, oiled frypan.
- Place steaks on serving plates, top with sautéed prawns and bearnaise sauce. Garnish with cracked pepper, if desired, and accompany with salad or vegetables of your choice.

Serves 4

This recipe is best prepared as required.

Margherita pizzas

1

2 large pizza bases with sauce

2

250g mozzarella cheese

3

250g cherry tomatoes, sliced

- Place pizza bases on oven trays. Cut mozzarella into thin slices and arrange over pizza bases, with the tomatoes.
- Bake in a 220C preheated oven for 15 minutes or until pizza bases are crisp and topping is lightly browned. Garnish with fresh herbs, if desired.

Makes 2 large pizzas.

Vegetarian korma noodles

1
250g dried egg noodles

2
400g packet fresh stir-fry vegetables

3
180g packet korma simmer sauce

- Cook noodles as directed on packet, drain, rinse under cold water and drain again.
- Add vegetables to a heated, greased wok or large frypan, stir-fry for 1–2 minutes, then stir in korma sauce and ½ cup of water and bring to the boil.
- Add cooked noodles to wok, mixing gently over heat until noodles are coated with sauce and heated through. Serve topped with natural yoghurt and garnish with coriander, if desired.

Serves 4-6

Italian grilled chicken fillets

1
4 small chicken fillets

2
150g marinated, char-grilled capsicum, cut into thick strips

3
125g mozzarella, sliced

- Pan-fry or grill chicken fillets until just cooked through. Place chicken fillets on an oven tray, top with char-grilled capsicum and mozzarella slices.
- Place under a preheated grill until mozzarella is bubbling and lightly browned. Serve with salad of your choice.

Serves 4

Sage and proscuitto turkey roll

1
**1kg turkey
breast roll**

2
**6-8 thin slices
prosciutto**

3
**¼ cup fresh
sage leaves**

- Thaw turkey breast roll* according to directions on box.
- Lay prosciutto slices on a chopping board, overlapping them slightly. Sprinkle sage leaves over the prosciutto. Carefully remove turkey roll from foil wrapping, place onto prosciutto then roll up in prosciutto and secure with toothpicks. Place turkey roll in a baking paper-lined baking dish, spray with cooking oil spray and cover with foil.
- Bake in a 180C preheated oven for 1 hour. Remove foil covering from baking dish, brush any pan juices over turkey roll then return to oven and bake uncovered for a further 30 minutes until golden. Remove turkey roast from oven, cover and rest in a warm spot for 10–15 minutes. Carve into slices and accompany with gravy and vegetables of your choice.

Serves 6-8

This recipe is best prepared as required.

*Frozen turkey breast rolls are available in supermarket freezers.

Barbecue chicken and sweet potato roast

1

1kg orange sweet potato

2

6-8 chicken thigh cutlets (with skin on)

3

MasterFoods Barbecue Smokey Seasoning

- Cut sweet potatoes into chunky slices, about 2–3 cm thick.
- Place chicken thighs and sweet potato in a large, greased roasting dish, spray with cooking oil spray and sprinkle liberally with barbecue seasoning.
- Bake in a 190C preheated oven for 40–45 minutes or until chicken is golden and cooked through and sweet potato is tender. Garnish with fresh herbs and serve with lemon wedges and steamed greens.

Serves 4-6

Baked Thai chicken

1
2 tblsp red Thai curry paste

2
165ml can coconut milk

3
4 chicken breast fillets, with skin on

- Mix curry paste with coconut milk in a large shallow dish. Add chicken breasts, turning to coat well in curry mixture. Cover and refrigerate for several hours.
- Remove chicken from marinade, place on a baking-paper lined oven tray and bake in a 180C preheated oven for about 25 minutes or until lightly browned and cooked through. Serve with lime wedges and Asian vegetables of your choice.

Serves 4

Dinner

Greek lamb with beetroot dip

1
MasterFoods Greek Seasoning

2
600g lamb steaks

3
200g tub beetroot dip

- Sprinkle seasoning generously over lamb steaks.
- Cook seasoned lamb steaks in a heated, greased large non-stick frypan or on a barbecue plate until cooked to your liking.
- Serve steaks topped with beetroot dip and accompany with vegetables or salad of your choice.

Serves 4

Roasted garlic and mushroom penne

1
300g cup mushrooms, sliced

2
500g pasta sauce with roasted garlic and wine

3
500g penne pasta

- Sauté mushrooms in a lightly oiled, large non-stick frypan until light golden. Add the pasta sauce and bring to the boil. Reduce heat and simmer uncovered for about 5–10 minutes.
- Cook penne pasta in a large pan of boiling water until al dente and then drain. Serve penne topped with the mushroom sauce and accompany with shaved parmesan, if desired.

Serves 4

Ginger and soy glazed pork

1
500g pork loin steaks

2
⅓ cup ginger marmalade

3
1 tblsp soy sauce

- Pan-fry steaks in a heated, lightly greased non-stick frypan for 3–4 minutes on each side until just cooked through. Remove from pan.
- Add marmalade, soy sauce and 2 tablespoons of water to frypan, stir over heat until mixture comes to the boil. Simmer for 2 minutes, then return chops to pan, turn to coat in glaze and heat through. Serve with noodles and Asian greens.

Serves 4

Lamb with balsamic onions

1
2 large onions

2
2 tblsp balsamic vinegar

3
12 lamb cutlets

- Place onions in a heated, oiled frypan and cook over a low heat until softened. Stir in balsamic vinegar and 1 tblsp water, simmer gently for 5–10 minutes.
- Meanwhile, cook cutlets in a separate frypan until browned on both sides and cooked to your liking. Serve cutlets topped with balsamic onions and accompany with vegetables of your choice.

Serves 4-6

Veal rolls with mozzarella and char-grilled vegetables

1

6 veal schnitzel steaks

2

200g char-grilled vegetables, drained

3

100g sliced mozzarella

- Pound steaks lightly with a mallet until even in thickness. Place a row of char-grilled vegetables across one end of each veal steak, then top with mozzarella. Roll up to enclose the filling and secure with toothpicks.
- Season rolls with salt and pepper, then pan-fry in a heated, oiled, non-stick frypan until browned all over.
- Reduce heat and cook over a medium heat for a further 6–8 minutes or until cooked through, turning occasionally. Lift rolls from pan and remove toothpicks. Serve with vegetables or salad of your choice.

Serves 4-6

Veal rolls can be prepared several hours ahead. Keep refrigerated and cook as required.

Oven-baked pumpkin frittata

1
1kg butternut pumpkin

2
8 x 59g eggs

3
150g tub roasted red capsicum, pecorino, cashews and basil dip

- Peel pumpkin, then remove seeds and cut into approximately 1.5cm cubes. Spread over a baking paper-lined oven tray, spray with cooking oil spray and season with salt and pepper. Bake in a 190C preheated oven for 20–25 minutes or until lightly browned and just tender.

- Transfer roasted pumpkin cubes to a 18cm x 28cm rectangular ovenproof dish.

- Whisk the eggs and dip together in a large bowl, then pour mixture over pumpkin in ovenproof dish. Bake in a 180C preheated oven for 25 minutes or until set and lightly browned. Accompany with a leafy salad.

Serves 6

Spicy sausages and beans

1

500g Italian-style sausages

2

680g jar pasta sauce with roasted garlic and onion

3

400g cannellini beans, drained

- Grill or pan-fry sausages until evenly browned and cooked through. Drain on paper towel, cool slightly, then slice diagonally.
- Place pasta sauce, cannellini beans and ½ cup of water in a large pan, stir over heat until mixture comes to the boil. Reduce to a simmer, add sliced sausages and simmer for a further 2–3 minutes to heat through. Serve with mashed potato.

Serves 4

Steak with Worcestershire cream sauce

1

4 scotch fillet steaks

2

⅓ cup Worcestershire sauce

3

300ml thickened cream

- Pan-fry steaks in a heated, lightly greased, non-stick frypan for about 4 minutes on each side or until cooked to your liking. Remove steaks from pan and rest in a warm spot.
- Add Worcestershire sauce to frypan, bring to the boil, then stir in cream and reduce heat. Simmer uncovered 5–6 minutes until reduced and thickened slightly. Serve steak with Worcestershire cream sauce and accompany with vegetables of your choice.

Serves 4

Baked lamb chops with olives

1

6 lamb chump chops cup pitted

2

kalamata olives

3

500g jar pasta sauce with oven-roasted garlic and wine

- Trim fat from chops. Pan-fry until browned on both sides then transfer to an ovenproof dish.
- Sprinkle olives over chops then pour over the pasta sauce. Cover dish and bake in a 180C preheated oven for 30–40 minutes or until chops are tender.
- Garnish with fresh basil leaves, if desired, and accompany with vegetables or salad of your choice.

Serves 4-6

Chilli pork cutlets

1
⅓ cup Asian-style salad dressing

2
1-2 tsp chilli flakes

3
4 pork cutlets

• Mix salad dressing with chilli flakes in a large shallow dish. Add pork cutlets and turn to coat well in marinade. Cover and refrigerate for at least 2 hours.

• Remove cutlets from marinade and grill, fry or barbecue for about 4 minutes on each side or until evenly browned and cooked through. Serve with vegetables or salad of your choice.

Serves 4

Lime and chilli salmon

1
4 salmon fillets

2
1-2 tsp crushed chilli

3
4-6 kaffir lime leaves, finely shredded

• Place salmon fillets in a shallow dish, add chilli and lime leaves and rub over salmon. Cover and refrigerate 1 hour.

• Cook salmon in a lightly oiled non-stick frypan or on a barbecue plate over a medium heat for about 3 minutes each side until browned or until just cooked through. Serve with rice and vegetables, and accompany with lemon or lime wedges.

Serves 4

Dukkah-crusted lamb
with beetroot

1
8-10 lamb cutlets

2
¼ cup dukkah, approximately

3
beetroot dip

- Coat the cutlets with dukkah, pressing it on firmly with fingertips.
- Cook cutlets in a heated, lightly oiled frypan over a medium heat until golden brown on both sides and cooked to your liking. Serve topped with beetroot dip and accompany with vegetables or salad of your choice.

Serves 4

Pork chops with roast cherry tomatoes

1
6 mid-loin pork chops

2
Masterfoods All Purpose Seasoning

3
300g truss cherry tomatoes

- Season chops well with the seasoning. Heat a baking dish on the stove and grease with a little oil or cooking spray. Add chops and brown on both sides.
- Remove baking dish from heat, add tomatoes then transfer to a 200C preheated oven and bake for 15–20 minutes or until chops are cooked through. Serve chops with vegetables of your choice.

Serves 4-6
This recipe is best prepared as required.

Zucchini and fetta pappardelle

1
3 large zucchini

2
375g packet pappardelle

3
350g tub marinated fetta

- Cut zucchini into thin ribbons with a vegetable peeler. Cook pasta in a large pan of boiling water until al dente, drain.
- Drain fetta, reserving 2 tablespoons of oil marinade. Heat 1 tablespoon reserved oil marinade in pasta pan, add zucchini ribbons, sauté 1–2 minutes, then add pasta, fetta and remaining oil marinade. Toss over heat to combine and heat through. Serve straightaway.

Serves 4
This recipe is best prepared as required.

Ginger teriyaki fish fillets

1

**4 thick white
fish fillets**

2

**3cm piece fresh ginger,
cut into thin strips**

3

**½ cup teriyaki
sauce**

- Cook fish fillets in a heated, lightly oiled non-stick frypan for about 3 minutes on each side or until just cooked through. Carefully remove fish from pan and keep warm.
- Add ginger strips to same frypan, sauté 1 minute, then stir in teriyaki sauce and simmer for 2–3 minutes until reduced and thickened slightly.
- Serve fish with ginger teriyaki sauce and accompany with rice and steamed Asian greens of your choice.

Serves 4

Cheese and chutney lamb cutlets

1

12 lamb cutlets

2

**4 thin slices
Jarlsberg cheese**

3

fruit chutney

- Grill or pan-fry cutlets until cooked to your liking.
- Cut each cheese slice into three pieces.
- Place cutlets on an oven tray, top each one with a teaspoon of fruit chutney and a piece of cheese. Place cutlets under a preheated grill and cook for a few minutes until cheese is melted. Serve with salad or vegetables of your choice.

Serves 4

Chorizo and zucchini sauce

1
500g fresh chorizo sausages

2
3 zucchini, thinly sliced

3
580g jar tomato and basil pasta sauce

- Pan-fry chorizo sausages in a heated, lightly greased frypan until evenly browned and cooked through. Transfer cooked sausages to a paper towel-lined plate and drain excess fat from frypan. Add zucchini slices to frypan and cook until tender and lightly browned.
- Slice drained chorizo sausages, return to frypan with pasta sauce, stir in ½ cup water and bring to the boil. Simmer 2–3 minutes until heated through. Serve with crusty bread, mashed potato, rice or pasta.

Serves 4

Sage and onion turkey schnitzel

1
500g turkey breast fillet steaks

2
1 extra large egg, lightly beaten

3
1½ cups sage and onion stuffing mix

- Place turkey steaks between two pieces of plastic wrap and pound with a meat mallet until thin. Cut turkey into 4 pieces.
- Lightly beat egg with 1 tablespoon water in a shallow dish. Dip turkey steaks in beaten egg then coat firmly with sage and onion stuffing mix.
- Shallow-fry crumbed turkey steaks in hot oil for 2–3 minutes on each side or until golden and cooked through. Serve with vegetables or salad of your choice.

Serves 4

Eggs and salmon en cocotte

1
200g tub crème fraiche

2
120g smoked salmon slices, roughly torn

3
4 x 59g eggs

- Lightly grease 4 x ¾ cup-capacity ramekins, place 1 tblsp of crème fraîche into each one, then top with smoked salmon and crack an egg on top. Add another tablespoon of crème fraîche to each ramekin and season with salt and pepper.
- Place ramekins into a baking dish and pour enough warm water into dish to come halfway up the sides of ramekins.
- Bake in a 180C preheated oven for 15 minutes or until eggs are just set. Remove ramekins from dish, garnish with dill and serve with toast.

Serves 4

Prosciutto and camembert chicken

1
4 small chicken breast fillets

2
125g camembert cheese, sliced

3
4 thin slices prosciutto

- Cut a slit along the side of each chicken fillet to form a pocket. Fill pockets with sliced camembert.
- Wrap a prosciutto slice around each breast and secure with a toothpick.
- Panfry the chicken fillets in a heated, lightly oiled non-stick frying pan for about 2 minutes on each side or until light golden. Transfer to a baking paper-lined oven tray and bake in a 180C preheated oven for 10–15 minutes until chicken is cooked through. Serve with vegetables or salad.

Serves 4

Lemon poached quince

1

2 large (1kg) quinces

2

1½ cups sugar

3

few strips lemon rind

- Peel quinces, cut them into small wedges and remove core.
- Place sugar, lemon rind and 1 litre water in large saucepan, add quince pieces and bring to the boil over a medium heat. Reduce heat and simmer quinces covered for 1–1½ hours until quince is very tender and deep rosy pink in colour.
- Lift quince pieces from syrup and place in a heat-resistant bowl. Return syrup to heat and boil for a further 15 minutes or until thickened slightly. Pour hot syrup over quince pieces. Serve warm or chilled as a dessert with custard, cream, yoghurt or ice-cream.

Serves 6

Caramelised apricot crepes

1

**600g (10)
fresh apricots**

2

**½ cup firmly packed
brown sugar**

3

**400g packet
(8) crepes**

- Halve apricots, remove stones and cut into wedges. Add apricot wedges to a greased, non-stick frypan and sauté for 1–2 minutes.
- Stir in brown sugar and $1/3$ cup water, and simmer 5–8 minutes or until apricots are tender and sugar caramelises to form a sauce.
- Warm crepes as directed on packet. Spoon apricots onto warm crepes, roll or fold up and drizzle with remaining caramel sauce. Serve with vanilla ice-cream or thick cream.

Serves 4

Dessert

Fruity baked apples

1

4 Granny Smith apples

2

fruit mince

3

½ cup apricot nectar

- Remove cores from the unpeeled apples using an apple corer. Cut a small piece from each apple core and place back into the base of apple to form a plug. Score through the skin around the centre of the apples with a small sharp knife.

- Fill the core cavity with fruit mince. Stand the apples in a greased ovenproof dish, pour apricot nectar around apples. Bake uncovered in a 180C preheated oven for 35–45 minutes or until apples are just tender. Serve with cream or ice-cream.

Serves 4

Toblerone mousse

1

**2 x 100g
Toblerone bars**

2

**300ml thickened
cream**

3

3 eggwhites

- Break Toblerone into pieces, place in a heat-resistant bowl and stand over a pan of gently simmering water until melted, stirring occasionally. Remove bowl from heat and cool slightly.
- Beat cream in a bowl with an electric mixer until soft peaks form. Beat eggwhites in a separate bowl with clean beaters until soft peaks form.
- Quickly fold whipped cream through melted Toblerone, then fold in beaten eggwhites. Pour mixture into 4 dessert glasses and refrigerate for several hours or until set. Serve sprinkled with extra chopped Toblerone, if desired.

Serves 4

Toffee affogato

1

8 sponge finger (Savoiardi) biscuits

2

English toffee ice-cream

3

1 cup hot freshly brewed black coffee

- Break biscuits into small pieces and divide between 4 serving glasses.
- Add 2 scoops of ice-cream to each glass, drizzle with hot coffee and serve straightaway.

Serves 4

Quick peach melba

1

425g can raspberries in syrup

2

4 large slipstone peaches, cut into wedges

3

1 litre premium vanilla ice-cream

- Puree the undrained raspberries in a blender or food processor until smooth. Press puree through a sieve to remove seeds. Serve peach wedges with ice-cream and raspberry puree.

Serves 4-6

Mango yoghurt meringue

1
4 meringue shells

2
large tub yoghurt with passionfruit*

3
2 bananas, sliced

- Roughly crush the meringue shells. Place half the crushed meringue over the base of four dessert glasses, top with half the yoghurt and half the banana slices. Repeat layers with remaining meringue, yoghurt and banana slices.

Serves 4

This recipe is best prepared as required.

* Yoghurt with passionfruit pulp is available from fresh food markets, salad and juice bars and some supermarkets.

Choc hazelnut cannoli

1
400g full-cream ricotta

2
100g hazelnut chocolate, grated

3
180g packet (20) mini cannoli shells

- Place ricotta in a bowl and gently stir in grated chocolate. Spoon mixture into a piping bag fitted with a 1.5cm plain nozzle.
- Pipe ricotta mixture into cannoli shells. Serve dusted with a little sifted icing sugar, if desired.

Makes 20

Warm cherry syrup cakes

1

425g can pitted black cherries in syrup

2

340g packet golden buttercake mix

3

2 tsp cornflour

- Drain the cherries and reserve syrup. Grease a 12 x 1/3-cup capacity non-stick muffin pan and line base of each hole with a round of baking paper. Divide cherries evenly between muffin holes.
- Make up cake mix as directed on packet, and then divide batter evenly over the cherries in muffin pan. Bake cakes in a 180C preheated oven for about 20–25 minutes or until cakes are just firm in centre.
- Meanwhile, blend the cornflour to a smooth paste with a tablespoon water. Combine the cornflour paste and reserved cherry syrup in a saucepan and stir over medium heat until sauce boils and thickens. Turn cakes out from pan onto serving dishes. Serve with cherry syrup and accompany with cream or ice-cream, if desired.

Makes 12

Mango in lime syrup

1

2 limes

2

½ cup sugar

3

**2 large
mangoes, sliced**

- Peel a few pieces of rind from limes with a vegetable peeler, remove any white pith, then cut rind into very fine strips. Squeeze limes and strain juice.
- Place the lime juice, sugar and ⅔ cup water in a small saucepan. Stir over a low heat until sugar is dissolved, then increase heat and boil for 5–7 minutes until syrup has thickened slightly. Remove syrup from heat and cool.
- Place mango slices and lime strips in a bowl, add syrup and refrigerate until well chilled. Serve with ice-cream.

Serves 4

Cherry crème tarts

1

**2 sheets butter puff
pastry, thawed**

2

**250g tub crème
fraîche**

3

**700g jar morello
cherries, drained**

- Cut each pastry sheet into 4 rounds, using a 10cm round cutter. Place rounds onto baking paper-lined oven trays. Press a 7cm round cutter lightly in centre of pastry rounds, without cutting all the way through, to create a border.
- Spoon crème fraîche over marked round on pastry, then top with cherries. Bake in a 190C preheated oven for 10–15 minutes or until pastry is golden. Serve dusted with sifted icing sugar, if desired.

Makes 8

Dessert

Blood orange jellies

1
½ cup caster sugar

2
1 tblsp gelatine

3
1¾ cups strained blood orange juice

- Grease 6 x ½-cup moulds with cooking oil spray.
- Place sugar and gelatine in a saucepan, add ¾ cup boiling water and stir over a low heat until sugar and gelatine are dissolved. Remove from heat and whisk in orange juice. Transfer mixture to a jug and pour into prepared moulds.
- Place moulds on a tray and refrigerate for several hours or until jellies are set. Carefully turn jellies onto serving plates. Serve with thick cream and blood orange segments, if desired.

Serves 6

We used Redbelly blood oranges in our recipe. They have a unique citrus-berry flavour and are available from August to October.

Black forest ice-cream

1
680g jar Morello cherries in syrup

2
3 tsp cornflour

3
cookies and cream ice-cream

- Drain cherries and reserve syrup. Place cornflour in a saucepan and blend to a smooth paste with a little of the reserved syrup.
- Stir in the remaining reserved syrup and cherries. Cook over a medium heat, stirring constantly until mixture boils and thickens slightly. Serve cherry sauce warm or chilled over cookies and cream ice-cream.

Serves 6

Blueberry lemon tartlets

1
54g packet (12) mini sweet tartlet cases

2
½ cup lemon curd, approximately

3
½ cup fresh blueberries, approximately

- Fill tartlet cases with lemon curd and top with blueberries. Dust with sifted icing sugar, if desired.

Makes 12

Dessert

Berry meringue ice-cream cake

1
100g meringue nests, roughly crushed

2
1 litre boysenberry ice-cream, slightly softened

3
300g frozen mixed berries

- Line an 11cm x 21cm loaf pan with enough plastic wrap to cover base and extend over side of pan. Reserve about ½ cup of the crushed meringue.
- Place boysenberry ice-cream, frozen mixed berries and the remaining crushed meringue in a large bowl, mix to combine. Spoon mixture into prepared loaf pan, sprinkle top with reserved meringue and place in the freezer for several hours or overnight until firm.
- Lift ice-cream cake from pan, remove plastic lining and transfer to a serving plate.

Serves 8-10

Ginger crunch apricot yoghurt

1
125g gingernut biscuits

2
825g can apricots in juice, drained

3
550g tub creamy vanilla yoghurt

- Process the gingernut biscuits in a food processor until roughly crushed or place in a plastic bag and crush with a rolling pin.
- Puree the apricots in a food processor until smooth. Layer yoghurt, apricot puree and crushed gingernuts in 4 dessert glasses. Refrigerate for 30 minutes before serving.

Serves 4

Hokey pokey ice-cream sandwiches

1
**2 litres vanilla
ice-cream**

2
**3 x 50g chocolate-
coated honeycomb
bars, chopped**

3
**250g pkt
chocolate
ripple biscuits**

- Place vanilla ice-cream in a large bowl, allow it to soften slightly, then stir in chopped honeycomb bars.
- Line a 20cm x 30cm rectangular pan with plastic wrap to cover base and extend up sides of pan. Spread ice-cream into lined pan, cover and freeze overnight until firm.
- Working quickly, lift the hokey pokey ice-cream from pan and cut into rounds with a 6cm cutter. Sandwich each ice-cream round between 2 chocolate biscuits, place on a tray, cover and return to freezer for several hours before serving.

Makes 13

Note: Any leftover hokey pokey ice-cream can be kept in the freezer and scooped into ice-cream cones to serve.

Dessert

Cheat's blueberry brûlée

1

**125g fresh or frozen
blueberries**

2

**500ml Premium
vanilla custard**

3

**2 tblsp caster
sugar**

- Divide the blueberries between 4 x ½-cup capacity ramekins.
- Spoon the custard over blueberries and smooth the top surface. Sprinkle sugar evenly over custard layer.
- Use a kitchen torch* to caramelise sugar topping until golden. If you don't have a kitchen torch, place dishes under a preheated grill and cook until sugar is caramelised.

Serves 4

*Kitchen torches are available from specialty kitchen shops.

Dessert

Jaffa cups

1

4 x 150g tubs vanilla bean frûche

2

finely grated rind and juice of 1 orange

3

200g dark chocolate, chopped

- Place frûche, orange rind and juice in a large bowl and stir to combine.
- Place chocolate in a heat-resistant bowl over a pan of simmering water and stir until melted (or microwave on medium for about 1½ minutes). Remove bowl from heat and cool to room temperature.
- Whisk half the frûche mixture into the melted chocolate, then add the remainder and whisk until well combined. Spoon into 6 small dessert glasses or little coffee cups and refrigerate for several hours until set.

Serves 6

This recipe is best prepared several hours ahead. Keep covered in the refrigerator.

Gingernut pears

1

10 (125g) gingernut biscuits

2

30g butter, melted

3

825g can pear halves, drained

- Process the gingernut biscuits in a food processor to form coarse crumbs. Transfer gingernut crumbs to a bowl and stir in melted butter.
- Place pear halves on a baking paper-lined tray and top with biscuit mixture. Bake in a 170C preheated oven for about 8 minutes or until lightly browned. Serve with cream or ice cream.

Serves 4-6

Hot cherry trifle

1

425g can pitted cherries in syrup

2

250g buttercake, cut into cubes

3

600ml prepared vanilla custard, warmed

- Place undrained cherries into a small saucepan. Bring to the boil then reduce heat and simmer uncovered for about 10 minutes or until syrup reduces and thickens slightly.
- Cut cake into 2cm cubes, divide between 4 dessert glasses, top with hot cherry mixture and warm custard. Serve straightaway.

Serves 4

Lamington ice-cream cake

1

1 litre strawberry ice-cream

2

350g packet (18) lamington fingers

3

125g strawberries, halved

- Line a 12cm x 22cm medium loaf pan with enough baking paper to cover base and extend up sides of pan. Spoon the ice-cream into a large bowl and allow to soften slightly.
- Layer half the lamington fingers over base of prepared pan, spread half the softened ice-cream on top. Repeat layers with remaining lamingtons and ice-cream. Cover mixture and freeze for several hours until firm.
- Using the lining paper, lift cake from the pan. Remove lining paper and transfer to a serving plate. Decorate top with sliced strawberries. Serve in slices.

Serves 8-10

Strawberry gelato

1

2 x 250g punnets strawberries

2

1 cup icing sugar

3

600ml thickened cream

- Blend strawberries and icing sugar in a food processor until smooth. Add the cream and process again until combined. Pour mixture into a 2-litre container and freeze for several hours or until firm.
- Chop up frozen mixture roughly and process in batches in food processor until smooth. Return processed mixture to a container and re-freeze overnight. Scoop gelato into small cups to serve.

Makes about 2 litres

Maple and pecan apples

1

**4 medium Granny
Smith apples**

2

½ cup maple syrup

3

**⅓ cup pecans,
toasted and chopped**

- Peel apples and remove cores with an apple corer. Cut apples into 1cm slices.
- Place apple slices in a large frypan, add the maple syrup and ½ cup water. Simmer uncovered for about 10 minutes until the apple is just tender and syrup has reduced and thickened, turning apple slices occasionally. Sprinkle the apple with toasted pecans and serve warm with vanilla ice-cream.

Serves 4

Caramel roast peaches with macadamia crumble

1
4 slip-stone peaches (or 8 canned peach halves)

2
⅓ cup brown sugar

3
8 macadamia butter shortbread biscuits, roughly crushed

• Cut peaches in half and remove stone. Place peach halves, cut-side up in a lightly greased ovenproof dish. Sprinkle with brown sugar and then with crushed biscuits. Bake in a 180C preheated oven for 10–15 minutes until sugar has caramelised and biscuit crumble is lightly browned. Serve with thick cream.

Serves 4-6

The caramel roast peaches are best prepared as required.

Cinnamon apple pancakes

1

**375g bottle Greens
pancake mix**

2

**1 medium green apple,
peeled and grated**

3

cinnamon sugar

• Prepare pancake mix as directed on bottle. Pour pancake mix into a large bowl and stir in grated apple. Pour ¼-cup quantities of apple pancake batter into a heated, greased, non-stick frypan, allowing room for spreading. Cook until bubbles form on the surface of the batter then turn pancakes and cook other side. Repeat with remaining batter

• Serve the apple pancakes warm, sprinkled liberally with cinnamon sugar. Accompany with cream or ice-cream, if desired.

Makes about 14